Behold!
The Word Is God

Hymns of Tukaram

Translated by Shanta Gokhale
and Jerry Pinto

SPEAKING
TIGER

SPEAKING TIGER BOOKS LLP
125-A, Ground Floor, Shahpur Jat
New Delhi—110049

First published by Speaking Tiger Books in paperback in 2023

ISBN: 978-93-5447-579-5
eISBN: 978-93-5447-572-6

10 9 8 7 6 5 4 3 2 1

Typeset in EB Garamond by SŪRYA, New Delhi
Printed at Shree Maitrey Printech Pvt. Ltd., Noida

CONTENTS

INTRODUCTION

Talking About Tukaram

In the sea of uncertainty that surrounds Tukaram's life and work, very few facts surface that we can hold on to as solid and incontestable. The culture of this great sub-continent has always shown a distinct lack of interest in history. Rather than recording mere facts, colourless and dry as they are, we have preferred to create legends and myths to move, awe and inspire people. Had it not been so, any member of Tukaram's family or circle of countless followers could, one imagines, have documented every detail of his life till the very day of his disappearance. That did not happen. As a result, scholars trying to put together an authentic account of his life have had to rely mostly on scattered biographical references in his abhangas and on the hagiography provided by Mahipati Taharabadkar, an eighteenth-century poet-saint from Ahmednagar.

Mahipati's verse chronicles recording the lives of saints came out some 125 years after Tukaram disappeared. By this time, the miracles and legends attributed to Tukaram were firmly established as facts in the hearts and souls of his followers. Even had he wanted to, Mahipati could hardly have been expected to question them. But we may safely assume that he did not want to. Saints were saints as much for the substantial work they did as for the divine powers they were supposed to possess.

The story repeats itself with Tukaram's abhangas. Perhaps an authentic manuscript in his hand did once exist. If it did, it has vanished. What we have instead are collections of scattered copies that some of his more diligent followers discovered when they combed Maharashtra looking for them. Presumably the copies were made from memory by Tukaram's accompanists and devotees, some of whom had become kirtankars themselves and made them part of their repertoire. We know this happened from what Tukaram's most ardent disciple, the sant-poet Bahinabai, says in her autobiography. She writes of the first time she heard an abhanga of Tukaram's from an itinerant kirtankar and found such depth in it that she became instantly obsessed by the desire to meet him and be accepted as his disciple. Her husband was thoroughly angered by this unwifely desire and sought to discourage her with various forms of punishment. But she remained undeterred. Finally, he allowed himself to be persuaded to move to Tukaram's village, Dehu, for some time where Bahinabai's cherished desire was granted. Tukaram accepted her as his disciple.

Considering the circumstances under which the abhangas we read today were retrieved, it is not surprising that even the four collections considered by scholars to be more or less authentic—the Dehu MS, the Kadusa MS, the Talegaon MS and the Pandharpur MS—are marred by inconsistencies. Spellings vary, abhangas vary, numbering varies. The most frustrating feature of all four is the absence of a chronological order. Modern editors basing their collections on one or other of the four gathas, have corrected the most glaring mistakes and attempted to eliminate abhangas that they suspect have been interpolated; but they have not imposed any order on the abhangas, having no authority to do so.

The very first compilation of Tukaram's abhangas in modern format was published by Indu-Prakash Press in 1873 (some date it at 1869) under the auspices of the colonial government of the Bombay Presidency. Some scholars claim this compilation used the Talegaon MS as its source. If so, that would be the work chiefly of one Trimbak Kasar, a Warkari from Talegaon Dabhade, who is said to have spent forty years travelling the length and breadth of Maharashtra picking up copies of abhangas wherever he could find them. At the end of his arduous search, he had collected over four thousand abhangas.

So far as Tukaram's life is concerned, some facts and events are accepted as unquestionably true. Tukaram was born in 1608 in Dehu, a small village on the banks of the river Indrayani. He was the second son of Bolhoba and Kanakai Ambile. The Ambiles were a branch of the More family. They were shudras by caste; but, besides tilling the large tract of fertile land they owned on the banks of the Indrayani, they practised another occupation that belonged properly to the vaishya caste. They ran a grocery shop, traded and lent money. They also held hereditary rights to the post of village mahajan. The mahajan was appointed to supervise other traders and collect revenue from them. This position gave the family a status that did not, as a rule, belong to shudras. As a member of a family of grocers and money-lenders, Tukaram had learnt to read, write and keep accounts very early in life. But he took his literacy further. He read widely, particularly religious texts like the Bhagvat and the writings of sant-poets.

Vitthala/Vithoba/Pandurang had been the family deity for generations. An ancestor had built a temple to Him on their land in the fourteenth century. Sant Dnyaneshwar had initiated the monotheistic worship of Vitthala as an incarnation of Vishnu. Devotees who made an annual pilgrimage to the Vitthal temple in Pandharpur came to be called Warkaris, the makers of the 'wari' or regular pilgrim trek. The Warkari sect which had lain dormant during the two following centuries when the Deccan was torn by wars, was revived by Tukaram, who made it a widespread movement for all castes and creeds.

Tukaram appears to have had a happy childhood, dearly loved by both parents. He was married when he was still an adolescent as was the practice then. His wife Rakhma came from his maternal uncle's family and he was very fond of her. They had a son called Santaji. However, Rakhma suffered from asthma and found it difficult to perform her family duties. So Tukaram's father married him to Awali, a girl from a well-off family, changing her name to Jija. It cannot have been fun for her to come into a large family as a second wife to a beloved first. Yet life was good till a series of misfortunes hit Tukaram. The first was the loss of both his parents within a few months of each other. The second was the death of his older brother Savji's wife. Savji had always been of an ascetic bent and his wife's death finally prompted him to leave home to become a sanyasi.

Thus suddenly, at the age of seventeen, Tukaram found himself at the head of the family, expected to manage its fields, shop, trading and money-lending interests. Although he had assisted his father in the fields and the shop from the time he was thirteen, the prospect of handling everything single-handed with no elder person to guide him was frightening. As it turned out, he managed the farming and the shop pretty well. But trade and money-lending appeared to defeat him. He was repeatedly gypped by local sharks, till stories about his naivete in business became the stuff of village gossip. Meanwhile, Jija was bearing children at the rate of one a year. By 1629, she was the mother of six.

This was the year when the third and worst calamity of Tukaram's life hit him. For two years not a drop of rain fell. The Deccan suffered a drought the likes of which it had never experienced before. The entire plateau region lay waste. Rivers dried up, crops shrivelled, food ran out and animals and people alike died of starvation. All around was devastation and disease. Corpses piled up. It was a time when humanity itself became a casualty. A visiting historian, Abdul Hamid Lahori, recorded that the flesh of a son became more desirable now than his love. Rakhma, already weakened by asthma, died begging for food. Santaji followed. Tukaram was twenty-one. For four years he had managed, although not too successfully, to keep his head above water. But the famine knocked him right out. His fields thirsted, his business spiralled downwards, he borrowed money to keep it going, could not repay the loans and went bankrupt. The prestige that his family had enjoyed for centuries was now mud. Vitthal, whom the family had worshipped with single-minded devotion, appeared to have absented himself from their side. Tukaram had become a pauper. He went into a deep depression.

Seeking solace away from worldly duties, he retired to the nearby Bhandara Hill. Here, as he says in a famous abhanga, trees, creepers and birds became his family. There was no one to reproach him for his shortcomings. He had all the time in the world to think about Krishna's life and deeds, to be in dialogue with himself, to sort out the thorny problems of devotion and life. Some scholars believe that he began to compose abhangas after his sojourn on Bhandara Hill. He seems to have decided then that poetry was to be his path to Vitthal; that poetry was prayer and prayer, poetry. He saw himself as an inheritor of the legacy of sants like Dnyaneshwar, Eknath, Namdev and Kabir. He writes in a well-known abhanga that Namdev appeared to him in a dream and instructed him to complete the task that he himself had left incomplete (See page 33). Write poetry, said Namdev. Don't make excuses.

The Vitthal temple on the family's land had fallen into disrepair. When Tukaram returned from Bhandara, he reconstructed it and began to spend all his days there, performing kirtans regularly every Ekadashi day. Soon the verandah on which he performed kirtans before an ever-growing gathering of devotees from all over Maharashtra came to be known as Anand Ovari—the verandah of bliss. Kirtans were a form of group worship conducted through stories about Vitthal and songs in praise of the deity.

Tukaram's growing influence disturbed the local brahmins. They saw him as a rebel against the established Vedic religion in which the rituals they performed constituted the only path to God. That Tukaram should have the temerity to show common folk a direct path to God was his first offence. His second was writing in Marathi, not Sanskrit, the language of the gods. His third was the unpardonable offence of a shudra daring to speak of religion at all. Mambaji, the leader of the local brahmins in whose wada Bahinabai was staying, asked her angrily, 'How can knowledge exist in a shudra's brain?'

With Tukaram trampling on so much brahmin turf, there was bound to be retribution. The brahmins asked a scholar what punishment he would suggest for such a one as Tukaram. The scholar said to Tukaram, 'If you wish to avoid being ostracised, you must abjure your writings by sinking them in the Indrayani.'

Tukaram yielded to the demand. He immersed his manuscript in the river and then sat on the bank for thirteen days on a fast unto death. At the end of this period, his manuscript is supposed to have surfaced, intact. Tukaram's followers and detractors who had gathered on the riverbank witnessed the miracle. The brahmins conceded that the shudra was indeed divinely blessed. Later two of them became his devotees. Tukaram was now free to continue his life as before. But he did not. Perhaps he saw his ordeal-by-water which took place in 1645 when he was thirty-seven years old, as a sign that his work on earth was over. He began talking now about being called away to Vaikuntha, God's home.

At some point during the five years that intervened between the immersion of his manuscript and his disappearance, Tukaram was asked 'by sants' what had brought him to his present condition of withdrawal from the world. He answered the question with a long poem, the first lines of which are: 'I was born a shudra but engaged in business that belonged properly to vaishyas. Vitthal has been our family deity for generations. I have nothing to say about my life; but since you have asked, I will say that I have found no joy in it. I have had to bear many sorrows.' From here he goes on to recount the painful events of his life. This poem corroborates the story of his life as it has come down to us. Significantly, it differs in one part. Although Tukaram speaks of being compelled to drown his poems in the river and of fasting on its banks for thirteen days, he does not say a word about his manuscript floating up at the end of those thirteen days. Instead, he winds up his story with the lines, 'All my capital consists of what Pandurang directed me to say.' Tukaram was fairly rational in his approach to life. He was also extremely modest and not likely to claim divine powers. We can therefore happily conclude that his manuscript did not surface. The legend is a metaphorical way of saying that his abhangas survived despite their immersion. Which they did. On people's lips.

Tukaram disappeared in 1650 when he was forty-two. Where he went, what he did remains a mystery. The real mystery is why it has remained a mystery. It is not as though Tukaram had been secretive about his intentions. There are at least two abhangas in which he bids farewell to his followers. In the more famous of the two, 'Aamhi jaato aapulya gaavaa,' he says:

I am leaving for my home / It is time to say farewell
We were meant to meet in this place / Now we must part
I plead at your feet / Let compassion enter your heart
Greet visitors who happen by / With Lord Vitthal's name
Make Rama Krishna your daily chant / Tuka is on his way.

What were his followers doing when he sang this abhanga? Did they not take him seriously? Why did they not keep a vigilant eye on his every movement? Well, they did not. And so, we have a myth. He did not simply disappear. He was carried up to heaven in a chariot, surrounded by an aura of light. People witnessed this miracle at first hand!

It is easy to see why, despite the absence of an authentic collection of Tukaram's body of work, the abhangas still live on. They live on because the abhanga form lends itself perfectly to singing; and Tukaram's language is accessible enough for people to remember. An abhanga comprises a series of ovis, songs sung by women while grinding grain on the handmill. The meter of the ovi keeps time exactly with the rhythm of the work. The first set of three lines consist of six syllables each and accompany the first three rounds of grinding which are heavy and slow. By the fourth round, much of the grain has been ground and the stone wheel flies faster. The fourth line is therefore shorter, made of four syllables. Everybody knows the traditional melodies in which ovis are sung. So you have the glorious vision of thousands of Warkaris walking, running, singing and dancing to Pandharpur each year from every corner of Maharashtra. They have left all their cares behind. What they carry in their hearts now is unalloyed devotion. And bliss.

SHANTA GOKHALE

TRANSLATOR'S NOTE

What Tukaram Means to Me

Shanta Gokhale

First there was the Prabhat film *Sant Tukaram*. I saw it as a child. For years afterwards Vishnupant Pagnis who played Tukaram was the saint incarnate for me. My favourite song was '*Aadhi beej ekale*'.

> First there was a single seed.
> Sprouting, it became a sapling.
> The sapling grew into a tree.
> The tree birthed flowers and fruit by the thousand.

Later when I came to read Tukaram's abhangas, I could not find it in my parents' copy of the gatha. My father said it was the only abhanga in the film that was not written by Tukaram. The scales fell from my eyes. Were other things in the film equally untrue? Perhaps the scene that had upset me most wasn't true. It wasn't true that Jija had dragged her son through the village to the temple to show Tukaram how his children were suffering.

A few decades later, my father decided to retire, leave the city and live a rustic life in the environs of Pune. He spent every weekend for months looking for a plot that was large enough for a garden, a vegetable patch, a cowshed, a poultry house and a bungalow; and inexpensive enough for his middle-class pocket. He found one located in a dip of land in Talegaon Dabhade near to the *tala* (lake) that had given the village its name. Talegaon sat shoulder to shoulder with Tukaram's Dehu. Plot bought, my father spent every weekend for a year building a tiled bungalow of his own design. He called it 'Abhanga'. My parents' spacious bedroom had a wide picture window which framed Bhandara Hill on which Tukaram had spent days in contemplation after the great famine of 1629 had devastated his life. The bungalow was full of light and fresh air. The blue of the sky and green of the trees entered through every window, blurring the line between inside and outside.

Father did not live very long after the great move. A mere eighteen months later he was gone. But it had been long enough for him to welcome three grandchildren into 'Abhanga'. One was my daughter Renuka, whom he would fondly call Awali. Mother protested. Awali was a shrew. Surely he did not want to call his granddaughter that? Father said, 'You're wrong. Awali was an innocent girl. It was Jija who became a scold because of the rotten deal she got. But look how she fought. And brought up her children single-handed.' Mother withdrew her objections.

After Father's premature death, Mother found Tukaram for herself. A Warkari kirtankar, Manohar (Dada) Sabnis, used to come from Pune to Talegaon once a week to teach abhangas to a group of women in the village. Mother was not a religious woman, but, like her late husband, she loved music and poetry. She found both in the abhangas Dada taught. Unlike other bhajan teachers, he did not compose them in modern or classical melodies. He kept to the simple, traditional tunes that Warkaris sang and that Mother loved.

When Mother relocated to Mumbai, she got a group of women together and started her own bhajan class at home, naming it Swanand Bhakti Mandal ('Bliss-in-self' devotion group). She invited Dada to come to Mumbai once a month to teach the group. Dada would stay with us for two days, teach and leave. Mother would record the abhangas he taught on her tape recorder, practice them through the week and rehearse them with the group. Tukaram filled the air and we sang his verses as well as the Swanandis. The Swanand Bhakti Mandal continued to assemble even as Mother lay on her death bed. And they were there to sing her a farewell abhanga the day she died.

The injunction to translate the best in Marathi literature came to me from Mother when I was sixteen. Yet I would never have dared touch Tukaram had it not been for Jerry saying to me one day that he would like to translate him. Jerry carried away my Tukaram gatha that evening, and a few weeks later, sent me a list of 25 abhangas that he had selected. I went through the gatha and selected 26 more, including all of my mother's favourites. Jerry's idea was that we should translate them jointly. I thought we should do them separately, creating two versions for every abhanga. It would make an interesting jugalbandi—one bandish, two distinct voices singing.

Like all great writers and poets, Tukaram calls for multiple translations. Abhangas are written in the ovi metre in which lines are necessarily compact. With Tukaram they are also dense with hidden layers of meaning. Each translator would have her/his own way of unpacking them. It was for this reason that I felt two independent translations rather than a joint one might give readers a better idea of the original.

Moreover, Jerry is a poet. I am not. I assumed that he, as

today's practitioner of Tukaram's art, might want to do what Arun Kolatkar and Dilip Chitre had done in their translations of Tukaram—recast the abhangas as independent poems that ran parallel to his. My aim as a translator on the other hand, was not to take any liberties but to run as close as I could to the sense, movement, rhythm and form of the originals.

However, in translating the present selection of 51 abhangas, I felt defeated again and again by the sheer weight of the ideas that Tukaram implies but leaves unsaid and the sweet musicality of his language, so difficult to transfer to English. The consonants in English resist flow; the open vowels of seventeenth-century Marathi are made for fluidity. Words like 'maooli' are enveloped in soft shades of emotion that 'mother' simply does not evoke. Words like 'triputi' signal metaphysical concepts that have no equivalent in Western philosophy. As one crawled through these brambles, one had to be careful to keep the precious poems in one's arms unscathed.

Tukaram's abhangas, copied by many hands and gathered over many years, fall into no particular order, natural or otherwise. Secretly we are always looking for order. As translators, editors and tellers of stories, we were keen to give our selection a narrative order that would allow readers a view of the abhangas beyond their immediate sense. We realized that our selection fell into three overlapping but distinct groups—Tukaram and poetry, Tukaram and life and Tukaram and Vitthala. We have arranged the abhangas accordingly.

TRANSLATOR'S NOTE

Meeting the Saint

Jerry Pinto

I met Sant Tukaram for the first time in Standard VIII, Victoria High School, Mahim. One of his abhangas was part of our Marathi curriculum in the Maharashtra state syllabus. I do not even remember anyone telling me it was an abhanga or that it might be sung. (I would have thought, I suspect, as a twelve-year-old boy, that this was something that girls did because at my sister's school, Canossa Convent, the female students learned almost all their Hindi and Marathi poems by singing them together and individually.) To me—and, I think, to most of the other boys in my class—it was less a poem than a part of the syllabus. And as such, it was an imposition, another part of a meaningless jigsaw that our school teachers foisted on us. We had no idea what we were supposed to do with all these bits and pieces—the valency of Calcium, the sine of the angle of incidence, the subordinate adverb clause of reason, the racemose inflorescence, the causes and consequences of the Battle of Buxar. We simply did as we were told: we learned how to draw the slipper animalcule, we bisected angles and we memorised the principal products of places. As for this poem by Sant Tukaram, we suspected that it had something to do with God because He was referred to in the end and therefore it seemed to be a moral lesson. We didn't care much for moral lessons.

Or for poems.

The latter, we tied to chairs with rope, as Billy Collins says in his oft-quoted 'Introduction to Poetry', and tortured confessions out of them.

> 'They begin beating it with a hose
> to find out what it really means.'

We were equal opportunity torturers. We did that to William Wordsworth and to Maithili Sharan Gupt and to Sant Tukaram. We reduced their poetry to prose and we learned that prose by heart to answer questions in the examinations. We were also made to recite aloud, yes, but if we experienced the rhythm and music of language, it was by accident. Otherwise recitations were reduced to an awful test of memory; we were asked, for instance, to recite 'Verse 7 and 12 of Lord Ullin's Daughter,' and if we bungled them up, we were caned and, worse still, we failed our 'orals'.

It is a miracle that they didn't beat all the poetry out of us.

*

And yet, in the same school, with the same curriculum, with the same teachers, I found that I wanted to be a poet. I even tried my hand at writing but found I had nothing to say.

I began reading poetry seriously only in college. And then I came across Auden's injunction to young poets, to learn hundreds, thousands of lines by heart. I thought: Well, I have a head-start. I knew poems in English, Hindi and Marathi. (And one in French.) And on a long walk from Nariman Point to Malabar Hill, which took about two hours, I tried to recite all the poems I remembered, going from Subhadra Kumari Chauhan's *Khoob ladi mardani* to James Shirley's *Death the Leveller*.

Oddly enough, *Je kaa ranjale-gaanjale* surfaced.

I could say it all, or almost all of it. I still had no idea what it meant, except that someone's mind was as soft as butter. I think now it was onomatopoeia that saved Sant Tukaram for me; I love the scrape of 'ranjale-gaanjale', the way those 'nuh's and 'juh's scratch against each other, the way they sound like worn-out people, old people, their joints creaking, ranjale-gaanjale...

At around the same time, I began to see how Sant Tukaram loomed large for other people. I knew he was important because Amar Chitra Katha number 68 was devoted to his life. This too I read as I read all comics, enjoying the ease of it, the conversation between word and image. I was uninterested in the moral values espoused or the authenticity or inauthenticity of the material. For example, I read a weekly evangelical magazine called *Soldiers of God* with as much interest because it had a section in which an improving story was told in pictures. What it was about didn't matter; it was something to read. It was a comic.

After this I saw *Sant Tukaram*, the film (directed by Sheikh Fattelal—mark that name—and Vishnupant Damle, 1936) and again, I saw the film as I saw other films. This was a black-and-white classic and so it needed respectful attention and no popcorn. But that was it.

*

My copy says it was 1991 when *Says Tuka*, Dilip Chitre's versions of Sant Tukaram's abhangas, came out. That doesn't seem credible. These translations seem to have been around forever. Another confession: I read the book as I read other books of poetry. I did not read it 'against'. I did not read it critically. Tukaram's music played somewhere deep in the background but by now '*Je ka...*' had been eclipsed by the hundreds of times I had heard the music from Keshav Vaman Bhole's soundtrack of the 1936 film. I knew somewhere that this music, this sentimental framing was Bhakti Lite; I could be comfortable here because no one really takes bhakti seriously at this level. It is just a beautiful idea because it belongs to someone else, it is happening to someone else; and we all know, with a touch of discomfort and schadenfreude mixed up, that this bhakti will ravage that someone else whoever she is. She will be ecstatic one moment and tormented the next. She cannot have one without the other.

But even on the level of language, I felt I was a tourist, I was seeing the sights. However, I was also a tourist who was intent on getting his money's worth.

So I thought I should ask a local. I asked Shanta Gokhale about Dilip Chitre's translations of Tukaram and she smiled her beautiful and compassionate smile and clicked her tongue.

'Do you think you could do a better job?' I asked.

'With one hand tied behind my back,' she replied with cheerful insouciance.

A remark that would come back to haunt her.

*

In 1991, I had no idea that I would ever translate anything other than my thoughts and those thoughts went into English. This seemed difficult enough, project enough. But things change and tongues change.

And one day I told Shanta Gokhale that I wanted to know

more about Tukaram. She gave me a Tukaram saarth and I bore it home with the decision that I would read an abhanga a day.

I did. I began by reading the shanksheps, the little summaries, at the bottom of the page but then I realized that I was reading a sunk-shape, an interposing voice, and I decided I would do without, go raw and ready for everything, trusting the sound of my own voice bringing Tukaram on the page into my ear. I was probably doing a bad job but I was doing it my way and that seemed better, clearer, cleaner.

I was charmed.

I was startled by a man who could talk to God and use scatological references without any concern for the person addressed. That level of familiarity, that level of trust, that level of heartspeech—I was fascinated. I was also disappointed that he could use the term 'Chandala' when he meant someone foolish, or that he often advised you never to have any truck with atheists.

*

By 2013, I found myself a translator, a title that seems easier to claim than writer and poet, but which actually should be twice as revered. (If not, think Tintin. Did you read Tintin in French? Did you read Asterix and Obelix in Italian? The Bible in Hebrew/Greek? What would we know of what we know if we did not have translators?)

I had also read the saarth through and had bumped into *Je ka...* again. And this time it was not just a poem, not a moral lesson, it was a radical restatement of what it meant to be human.

It was like meeting someone you thought you knew only to discover that she was quite different. But I was still reading for another sound, for another world-view.

Then came a chance encounter with Neela Bhagwat. I had graduated from my Marathi class with her and we were friends. I have told the story of the beginning of *The Ant Who Swallowed the Sun: The Abhangs of the Marathi Women Saints* (Speaking Tiger, 2021) in that introduction. After I had worked on an abhanga and Neela had approved it, I would read them to Shanta as well to see whether she approved.

And on one of those sant-soaked evenings, that conversation came back to me.

'Do you still think you could do a better Tukaram than Chitre?' I asked.

'Not better,' she said. 'I'd do it differently.'

'You should,' I said.

'No, you should,' she said. And then, 'We should.'

*

I thought she meant a collaboration. But she meant a jugalbandi—one Tukaram abhanga followed by two interpretations, hers and mine.

We were well into our work when suddenly one day Shanta expressed a doubt. She had re-read Dilip Chitre's introduction to *Says Tuka* and been overwhelmed by its scholarship. She wondered why we were taking on this onerous project when he had devoted a lifetime to it. What could we add to what he had done?

I mulled over the question seriously and wrote her a long email putting down the reasons why I thought we had set sail on the project in the first place, unasked and unbidden. Shanta thought my mail made a fine statement of purpose and asked me to include it in my introduction. So here it is:

'Why are we doing this? Because, as Dilip Chitre says, Tukaram belongs to the future. He does, and here we are in that future. Now it might be that Tukaram deserves better than us, more than what we are doing, a deeper incursion than ours. But this is what he has got right now. He will make do. Others will read our work perhaps and say: My gosh, how they skimmed. And perhaps angered or even inspired by that, they will dive deep. Perhaps that is the only reason for us to be doing this, to make someone so angry that they dedicate a life to the poems and bring out an even better translation.

So, my feeling is: We began this project without huge ambitions, we did not want to do something for Tukaram. We wanted, I suspect, to do something for ourselves in this experiment. We wanted to wander as Warkaris down this path.

And so, in the spirit of the beginning, we will tread lightly. We will write no scholarly introductions. We will be naked before our readers, talking solely and simply of our love of the music, the message. We will not set ourselves up as scholars. And we will then let the work set sail on the new river of publishing.

The thing about post-modernism is that it has taught us that we cannot predict the readings, we cannot foretell the responses. My encounters with the world of people who read translations has always been thorny; they are always wondering why you did what you did, why you chose what you chose, could you not have...

That's all right too.

That's what one signs up for.

I think we should go on as we have begun, in the spirit of adventure, in the spirit of looking, in the spirit of the jugalbandi which may throw up its own magic.'

And so here are two Tukarams. They come from different worlds, from different histories, from different genders, from different, different, different.

They are united by the love of music, the respect for the power of the word, the desire to bring to you a feast they have enjoyed.

Dive deep now. For could it be you who is meant to take that next great leap of faith?

NOTE ON THE TRANSLITERATION

One of the things that bothered us about Chitre's *Says Tuka* is that he never tells us which abhanga he has translated so you're groping in a dark Chitrescape, guessing at the original. We decided to have the original abhangas as well, in Roman transliterations. Read these poems aloud, please. Don't be shy. And here's a transliteration cheat sheet:

The 'e' at the end is always the e of the elephant who laid an egg.

The single 'a' at the end is the French diphthong sound of oe as in being a good oeuf. (This is not being overly educated. The only other reference we can offer is Middle English. Here's the first line of the prologue to *The Canterbury Tales*:

Whan that Aprille with his shoures sote...

Both 'Aprille' and 'sote' end with that sound, the 'a' at the end of a word. Like abhang*a*.)

The 'o' is the 'o' of gold. It is not the 'o' of 'golf'.

The double 'l' is used for the retroflex 'l'. This is the eternal stumbling block of the Marathi language. That and the retroflex 'na'. Don't get too hassled.

And finally, 'j' is used for a sound between the 'j' of judge but this magisterial fellow comes from Zanzibar. You have to find a sound between his post and his origin.

Let us not talk about the 'ch' which is not the 'ch' of church. It is the 'ch' of the 'tsch' variety and you can try but don't worry if you fail. Life, however, is unfair. There is a well-known academic whose family was not Marathi speaking. When she was very young, someone heard her enunciate the Marathi 'tscha' perfectly. The family was so proud of his achievement that whenever there was a guest, she was required to come out and perform her Marathi 'tscha'.

As Jerry will tell you, I gave him my saarth. Later, because I needed some Tukaram in my life, I bought another. Thus he worked from Gopalrao Govind Benare's edition and I worked from Diwakar Anant Ghaisas' edition.

SHANTA GOKHALE

JERRY PINTO

Part One

TUKARAM AND POETRY

Naamdeve kele swapnaamaaji jaage

Naamdeve kele swapnaamaaji jaage | Save Pandurang yeuniyaa 1.
Saangitale kaama karaave kavitva | Vaauge nimittya bolo nako 2.
Maap taaki salle dharili Vitthale | Thapatoni kele saavdhaana 3.
Pramaannaachi sankhyaa saange shata koti | Urale te shevati laavi Tukaa 4.

Namdev walked into my dream
With Pandurang by his side
'Wake up, Tuka,' Namdev said,
'No extra talk. Here's work for you.'
He slapped me awake.
Vitthal held the scales.
He piled his poems in.
'A billion were pledged.
Some remain. Tuka,
You do the rest.'

SHANTA GOKHALE

Namdev and Pandurang
Roused me from a dream.
Namdev said, 'Write poems. No excuses.'
Vitthal had a pair of scales.
Namdev put his poems in one pan.
'I owed You a billion poems.
Tuka will write the rest.'

JERRY PINTO

Santaanchi ucchhishte bolato uttare

Santaanchi ucchhishte bolato uttare | Kaaya mya gawhaare jaanaave he 1.
Vitthalaache naama ghetaa naye shuddha | Tethe maja bodha kaaya kalle 2.
Karito kavitva bobadyaa uttari | Jhanni majavari kopa dharaa 3.
Kaaya maajhi yaati nenno haa vichaar | Kaaya mi te phaara bolo nenne 4.
Tukaa mhanne maja bolavito deva | Artha guhya bhaava tochi jaanne 5.

My words are lifted from the tongues of saints
I can't pronounce even Vitthal's name
I'm a country bumpkin. Ignorant.
I make poems like a lisping child
Scold me for them. I don't mind.
Remember too my low-caste birth.
I'll say no more. That is enough.
Says Tuka:
God gives me words.
Their meanings, feelings, he alone knows.

SG

My songs are the leavings of the saints.
How could I even know these things?
I can't get the sound of his name right.
What do I understand?
These songs are a child's lispings.

You know my worth, you know my birth.
I need say nothing more.
Tuka says: His is the meaning.
His the sense.

JP

Naahi saro yeta jodilya vachani

Naahi saro yeta jodilya vachani | Kavitvaachi vaanni kushallataa 1.
Satyaachaa anubhava vedhi sattapanne | Anubhavaachyaa gunne rucho yete 2.
Kaay aagipaashi shrungaarile chaale | Potiche ukale kasaapaashi 3.
Tukaa mhanne yethe karaavaa ukala | Laagechi naa bola vaadhavuni 4.

Words strung together don't make the cut
Poetry speaks with the tongue of art.
It's all about truth, truthfully sought.
The truth of experience gives poems their weight.
The heat of fire melts ornaments
A touchstone reveals what lies at the heart.
Says Tuka:
No need for further talk.
It's here and now. Let's have it out.

SG

The right words in the right order?
That's not enough for poetry.

This goes beyond language.
This is a search for truth.

Only experience, real experience
Gives flavour, brings substance.

Fire will claim the fake.
Real gold will shine through.

Tuka says: You are what you need.
Use no less, say no more.

JP

Nakaa dantkathaa yethe saango konni

Nakaa dantkathaa yethe saango konni | Korade te maani bola konna 1.
Anubhava yethe paahije saachaar | Na chalati chaar aamhaapudhe 2.
Vara konni maani rasaall bolanne | Naahi jhaali mane vollakhi to 3.
Nivadi vegalle kshir aanni paanni | Raajhansa donhi vegallali 4.
Tukaa mhanne yethe paahije jaatiche | Yera gabaallaache kaaya kaama 5.

Don't bring us fables | Who cares for empty tales?
We demand hard experience | Cant won't sell.
Who wants a glib tongue | Ignorant of Him?
Water isn't milk | Even swans can tell.
Says Tuka:
This work is for seekers
Not for casual comers and goers.

SG

Don't come around with hoary old legends
Who needs these empty words?
It's real experience we seek.
These lies won't wash.
What price pretty words without real knowledge?
A swan can tell milk from water. Can you?
Tuka says: This is hard work.
Poseurs please excuse.

JP

Sahaja leellaa mi saakshi yaachaa

Sahaja leellaa mi saakshi yaachaa | Naye vanchu vaachaa aise jaale 1.
Upakrame vade nishabdaachi vaanni | Je kothe bandhani gumpho nenne 2.
Tamanaasi pari vevhaaraa vegallaa | Raviprabhaakallaa varte jana 3.
Tukaa mhanne yethe gelaa atishaya | Aaataa punhaa naye tonda daavu 4.

This comes to me with natural ease
I must not burden it with speech.
My work calls for a quiet tongue
Not words bound by prosody.
The rising sun banishes the night.
People hail it. Work by its light.
The sun remains detached from it.
Says Tuka:
Here goes wordy excess.
Never again show me your face.

SG

I seek the spontaneous:
That which is lost in speech.
So I say nothing about the source.

To free myself from the concrete,
I choose silence.

He lights up the darkness
But holds himself aloof

From the play of light.

Tuka says: Begone, excess.
Don't show me your face again.

JP

Aaamhaa ghari dhana shabdaanchicha ratne

Aaamhaa ghari dhana shabdaanchicha ratne | Shabdaanchicha shastre yatna karu 1.
Shabdachi aamuchyaa jeevaache jeevana | Shabda vaatu dhana janalokaa 2.
Tukaa mhanne paahaa shabdachi haa deva | Shabdechi gaurava puja karu 3.

Words are the jewels that fill our homes
Words the tools we put to the test
Words are our breath, life of our lives
The wealth we offer the world as gifts
Says Tuka:
Behold! The word is God
To honour the word is worship.

SG

Words, our wealth.
Words, our tools.
Words, life of our life.
Words, the wealth we offer the world.
Tuka says: The Word is God.
The Word be praised.

JP

Part Two

TUKARAM AND LIFE

Kaaya dhoraapudhe ghaaluni mishtaanna

Kaaya dhoraapudhe ghaaluni mishtaanna | Kharaasi lepana chandanaache 1.
Nako nako devaa khallaachi sangati | Rasa jyaa pangati naahi kathe 2.
Kaaya seja baaja maakadaa vilaasa | Aallankaaraa naasa karuni taaki 3.
Tukaa mhanne kaaya paajuni navaneeta | Sarpaa visha theeta amrutaache 4.

To put sweets before cattle is silly.
Or sandalwood paste on an ass.
God, I will not keep company
With those who abjure your name.
What is a bed to a monkey?
A toy to tear up, a game.
Says Tuka:
What's butter to a serpent
Who turns even nectar to poison?

SG

You would not offer an ox a sweet.
Nor anoint an ass to give it a treat.
A monkey will ruin a feather bed.
Why keep company with the wicked?
Tuka says: Snakes infuse venom into nectar
Why offer one fresh-churned butter?

JP

Dhekannaachi baaja gada

Dhekannaachi baaja gada | utarachadha kevhadi 1.
Hotaa taisaa kallo bhaava | Aalaa vaava antarichaa 2.
Boraamadhye ase aalli | Athollicha bhovati 3.
Potaasaathi vechi channe | Raajaa mhanne tonde mi 4.
Bedakaane chikhala khaavaa | Kaaya thaavaa saagara 5.
Tukaa mhanne taise aahe | Kaaya paahe tyaat te 6.

The bed is a mountain to a bug
Oh what a climb it makes!
A mind is hedged in thus
By what the senses say.
A worm sits in a seed
Around him is the seed
A man feeds on horse gram
Declares he is king.
The frog is happy in mud
The ocean is nothing to him.
Says Tuka:
That is how it is
What you see is all there is.

SG

To a bedbug, the bed is a mountain:
A long hard climb.
Is your mind that bedbug?

A worm inside a fruit
Takes the fruit to be the world.
Are you that worm?

To the famished, a gram is a feast.
A frog in the mud has no notion of the ocean.

Tuka says: Is what it seems what it is?
Then that is all it is.

JP

Sadaiva tumhaa avaghe aahe

Sadaiva tumhaa avaghe aahe | Haata paaya chaalaayaa 1.
Mukhi vaanni kaani keerti | Dolle murti dekhaavayaa 2.
Andha bahira tthakali kiti | Muki hoti paangulla 3.
Gharaa aagi laavuni jaagaa | Na palle to gaa vaachenaa 4.
Tukaa mhanne jaagaa hitaa | Kaahi aataa aapulyaa 5.

You are lucky. You have it all.
Hands to work, legs to walk,
Ears to hear, tongue to laud,
Eyes to gaze on the image of God.
Yet you go and beggar yourself.
Turn wilfully blind, lame and deaf.
How can such a man be saved
Who, having set his house ablaze,
Still sits within. Will not escape?
Says Tuka:
Awake,
Your good is at stake.

SG

Rejoice in your wholeness, rejoice.
Your limbs work, you can raise your voice
In praise of God. You can hear, you can see
The image of God. But many there be
Who have chosen to live as if they were blind

Or deaf or dumb or lame in the mind.
If a man sets fire to his own home
And won't run away, who can save him?
Tuka says: At least now, arise, awake
Do this for your own sake.

JP

Shuddhaashuddha nivade kaise

Shuddhaashuddha nivade kaise | Charma maasa bhinna naahi 1.
Kaahi adhika naahi unne | Kavannyaa unne devaasi 2.
Udaka bhinna ase kaaee | Voholla baavi saritaa naee 3.
Surya teje nivade kaaya | Rashmi rasaa sakallaa khaaya 4.
Varnnaa bhinna dudhaa naahi | Sakallaa gaayi saarakhe 5.
Karitaa bhinna naahi maati | Madakyaa gati bhinna naave 6.
Varte ekavidha agni | Naahi mani shuddhaashuddha 7.
Tukaa mhanne paatra chaada | Kinvaa visha amrut goda 8.

What is pure and impure? | Skin and flesh are the same
None is more, none less | God does not discriminate.
Water is no different | Whether in well or river.
The sun falls fair and square | On earth's every corner.
Milk is of one colour | No matter the cow, its colour
Clay is finally clay | Whether as pot or pitcher.
A furnace and a flame | Both are equally fire.
Says Tuka:
Forget the container.
Are the contents poison or nectar?

SG

When we share the same flesh, the same blood,
Who can tell the pure from the impure?

Stream, well, rivulet, pond, river
All water, the same water.

Does the sun choose where to shine?
His rays flood the entire Earth.

What matters the colour of the cow
When we know her milk is always white?

Name the earthen pot what you will
They're all made of the same clay.

Fire is one in all its forms.
No spark is purer than another.

Tuka says: Ignore the pot
Ask what's inside:
Poison or nectar?

JP

Kaaya karu poraa laagali chata

Kaaya karu poraa laagali chata | Dhari vaata deullaachi 1.
Saangitale neghe kaani | Duje mani Vitthala 2.
Kaama ghari na kari dhandaa | Yethe sadaa dushchita 3.
Aamache kulli navhate aise | Hech pise nivadale 4.
Laukikaachi naahi laaj | Maajhe maja paarikhe 5.
Tukaa mhanne narakaa jaane | Yaa vachane dushtaanchi 6.

Oh what is to be done | My boy has gone astray,
He is at the temple | Every single day.
Deaf to us, his ears | Hear only Vitthal's name.
At home he's glum | Sits idle, will not work.
Never was such a one | A madman, born to us.
The world may say what it will | He is not ashamed.
He has turned a stranger | Mine only in name.
Says Tuka:
Such evil complaints
Should send their speakers to hell

SG

'Is my boy mad or is he simple?
He's always headed to the temple.
He listens to no word of mine.
Vitthal's always on his mind.
He does no work, he's never at home;
And when he is, his mind does roam.

Our family never was this bad.
This one turned out to be mad.
He cares nothing for the world's opinion.
I find I have lost my son.'
Tuka says: Pay no heed to this dumbbell
He's surely on his way to hell.

JP

Saatthavilaa vaanna

Saatthavilaa vaanna | Paeesa ghaatalaa dukaana 1.
Je jyaa paahije je kaalli | Aahe siddhachi javalli 2.
Nivadile saache | Uttama madhyama kanishtthaache 3.
Tukaa baeesalaa dukaani | Daavi molaa aeesi vaani 4.

I've bought this roomy shop.
Stocked it well.
Here's everything you want.
I'm all set to sell.
There's something for every pocket,
Low, medium, best.
Tuka is in his shop.
Take what your money can fetch.

SG

New stock in. All new, all new.
In a fine shop for you to view.

What do you want? What's your demand?
It's all here. It's all to hand.

I have lots of the very best.
Okay stuff too. Yes, even the rest.

Tuka is in the shop.
What you get will depend
On the money you have to spend.

JP

Mana karaa re Prasanna

Mana karaa re Prasanna | Sarva siddhiche kaaranna 1.
Moksha athavaa bandhana | Sukha samaadhaan icchha te 2.
Mane pratima sthaapili | Mane mana puja keli 3.
Mane icchhaa puravili | Mana maauli sakallanchi 4.
Mana guru aanni shishya | Kari aapulechi daasya 5.
Prasanna aapa aapannaasa | Gati athavaa adhogati 6.
Saadhaka vaachaka pandita | Shrote vakte aeekaa maata 7.
Naahi naahi aana daeevata | Tukaa mhanne dusare 8.

Open up your minds | The home of all attainment
The very source of bondage | Freedom and contentment.
The mind is the idol | The mind is the prayer
The mind is the mother | Of all that is there
The mind is the teacher | The mind is the taught.
Master and slave | It serves and it commands.
The mind is your rise | The mind is your fall.
Heed me you seekers | Listeners, scholars, all.
Says Tuka:
There's no almighty
Above and beyond the mind.

SG

Mind, make me happy
You're the source of all resources.

Mind, the bonds.
Mind, the release.

Mind, just happiness.
Mind, the reflection.

Mind, the worship.
Mind, the completion.

Mind, my mother.
Mind, guru; mind, disciple.

Mind, slave-driver.
Mind, the solipsism.

Mind full speed ahead
Mind the dawdler.

Mind reader, mind scholar
Mind auditor, mind seeker.

Tuka says: It's all mind.
No other God.

JP

Aeekaa mahimaa aavadichi

Aeekaa mahimaa aavadichi | Bore khaaya bhillatichi 1.
Thora premaachaa bhukelaa | Haachi dushkaalla tayaalaa 2.
Pohe Sudama devaachi | Phake maari koradechi 3.
Na mhanne ucchhishta athavaa thode | Tukaa mhanne bhaktipudhe 4.

Listen to this great love story
The Bhil woman offered berries
Nibbled to test for bugs.
God, starved of love,
Devoured them all.
Sudama offered a gift—
A small pouch of pohe.
God ate whole fistfuls,
Uncooked, raw.
He did not say too little, half-eaten
Ate with delight what was given
Says Tuka:
It was love and devotion.

SG

This then is the miracle of love.
When a love famine rages in heaven.
God will take berries from a Bhil woman.

Sudama's gift of poha was slight.
Krishna wolfed it down with delight.
Tuka says: Half-eaten, a little, it matters not.
God will take what you've got.

JP

Chandanaache haata paayahi chandana

Chandanaache haata paayahi chandana | Parisaa naahi heena konni anga 1.
Deepaa naahi paathhi poti andhakaara | Sarvaangi saakara avaghi goda 2.
Tukaa mhanne taeesaa sajjanaapaasuna | Paahataa avagunna milechi naa 3.

Sandalwood is sandalwood in every limb
The touchstone is true, out and in
Light is light, back and front
Sugar is sweet in every grain
Says Tuka:
Hard as you might look
The good are good all through.

SG

Sandalwood is sandalwood is sandalwood.
The philosopher's stone brooks no impurities.

Light is light.
Light first.
Light afterwards.

Sugar is sweet
Through and through.

Tuka says: There can be no vice
In a man of virtue.

JP

Je kaa ranjale gaanjale

Je kaa ranjale gaanjale | Tyaasi mhanne jo aapule 1.
Tochi saadhu ollakhaavaa | Deva tethechi jaannaavaa 2.
Mrudu sabaahya navaneeta | Taeese sajjanaache chitta 3.
Jyaasi apangitaa naahi | Tyaasi dhari jo hrudayi 4
Dayaa karanne je putraasi | Techi daasaa aanni daasi 5.
Tukaa mhanne saangu kiti | Tochi bhagavantaachi murti 6.

He who says these are mine
Of those in torment and pain
Recognize him. He's a saint.
Recognize God's presence there.
Much like butter, the virtuous man
Is soft in every part.
Clasping closest to his heart
The neglected, the outcast.
His love makes no difference
Between son and servant
Says Tuka:
Why say more?
He is the divine incarnate.

SG

How do you tell a saint?
Look for such a one as takes for his own
The overborne, the outworn and the forlorn.

Know that this man is an image of God
His mind is as soft as butter, inside and out.
To his heart he holds the lowborn, the baseborn.
His slaves and his children are as one to him.
Tuka says: I can go on and on.
This is the embodiment of God.

JP

Deva hoeejeta devaache sangati

Deva hoeejeta devaache sangati | Patana pangati jagaachiyaa 1.
Dohikade donhi vaahaateela vaataa | Kariteela saathhaa aapulaalaa 2.
Daakhavile pari naahi varijitaa | Aalaa tochi chittaa bhaaga vari 3.
Tukaa mhanne angi aavadiche balla | Upadesha moolla beejamaatra 4.

Be with God, godliness is yours.
Be with the world, your fall is assured.
Two paths two ends, choose what you will
What use that I say, why that, choose this.
You will choose, that which you please
Says Tuka:
Counsel is but a seed
The force of the will is stronger still.

SG

Choose God and you choose godlike.
Choose the world and you choose worldly.

Two roads. Two directions.
Choose yours with care.

I've told you what I know.
Your choice, now. Consequences follow.

Tuka says: You must want God.
That's the secret. That's the seed.

JP

Chanchalli chanchalla nishchalli nishchalla

Chanchalli chanchalla nishchalli nishchalla | Vaajavi khallaalla udakaasi 1.
Sope varma pari mana naahi haati | Haa haa bhoota chitti bhrama gaadhhaa 2
Ravibimba naahi tutata udakaa | Chhayechi te nakaa sari dharu 3.
Tukaa mhanne bhaya dhari rajjusaathhi | Naahi saacha poti kallale to 4.

When the bed is deep, the stream is still;
When shallow, it rumbles and roils.
A thought perfectly easy to follow
If your mind is under control.
The unstill mind confounds
Object with fleeting shadow.
The sunbeam which pierces the stream
Is only the beam's reflection.
Says Tuka:
If you cannot tell false from true
A rope is a fearful snake to you.

SG

Are you the shallow stream
That runs over a rocky bed,
Burbling and babbling all the time?
Depth brings tranquility.

If our minds were at peace
If illusions weren't so pleasing
We would be able to tell

The real from the shell.
We'd see that the sunbeam
Never enters the stream.

Tuka says: If you can't tell the real from the fake
You'll scream when you take the rope for the snake.

JP

Sansaaraachaa maathaa bhaara

Sansaaraachaa maathaa bhaara | Kaahi para na thhevi 1.
Bhaktichi te jaati aeesi | Sarvasvaasi mukaave 2
Bhikshaa aanni vevasaava | Kaalaa kari to gaadhhava 3
Karuni vasati baajaari | Mhannavi kaasayaa nispruhi 4.
Prasaada aaduni kavi | Kele tupa paani tevi 5.
Tukaa mhanne hoee shoora | Kinvaa nisura majura 6.

Few can shed the burden—
The life of the world.
And here is devotion
That demands you give up all
Only an ass will mix
Ascetism with business.
Sitting in the market-place
Why claim that you are free?
Stealing a poet's words
Will not turn water to ghee
Says Tuka:
Choose your way
Be brave or remain a slave.

SG

You won't put it down, will you, no matter what?
But bhakti demands you set down all baggage.

Alms are one thing; the take is another.
Donkey, don't confuse them with each other.

You say you're free of desire; in a state of grace.
Why stake out space in the market-place?

Stealing a poet's words to mix them with yours?
You can't make ghee from water, defy nature's laws.

Tukaram says: Do you have the guts for this?
If not, go get some honest work.

JP

Parise ge sunebaaee

Parise ge sunebaaee | Nako vechu dudha dahi 1.
Aaavaa chaalili Pandharapuraa | Vesipaasuni aali gharaa 2.
Aeeke goshti saadara baalle | Kari jatana phutake paalle 3.
Maajhe haatichaa kalavadu | Majavaachuni nako phodu 4.
Vallavatakshirinche limpana | Nako phodu majavaachuna 5.
Ukhalla musalla jaate | Maajhe mana guntale tethe 6
Bhikshuka aalyaa gharaa | Saanga geli Pandharapuraa 7.
Bhakshi maapita aahaaru | Nako phaarisi varu saaru 8.
Soona mhanne bahuta nike | Tumhi yaatresi jaave sukhe 9.
Saasubaaee swahita joda | Sarva maageela aashaa soda 10.
Soonamukhiche vachana kaani | Aeekoni saasu vivanchani mani 11.
Savatiche chaalle khote | Myaa jaavese ilaa vaate 12.
Aataa kaasayaa yaatre jaau | Kaaya jaauni tethe paahu 13.
Mule lekare gharadaara | Maajhe yethechi Pandharapura 14.
Tukaa mhanne aeese jana | Goviyele maayekaruna 15.

Listen, says the mother-in-law | Don't finish the milk and dahi
On her way to Pandharpur | She turns at the village boundary.
Attend to what I say, my dear | My cracked wood pan needs care
The dung-cake stack I've made | Don't break it while I'm away.
That vermicelli is for kheer | Please don't touch the container
I'm so attached to my things | My quern, my pestle, my mortar.
If a sadhu stops by our gate | Say she's gone on pilgrimage.
Keep your diet moderate | Don't eat rich food. Don't gorge.
The daughter-in-law says, you are right. | Please go with easy mind.
Think only of your welfare | Not things you've left behind.
She hears the woman's words. | Her heart fills with unease.

She's up to some tricks, I'm sure | She wants me gone if you please
But I'll stay. Why go to Pandharpur? | What is there to see?
My home, my children, are here. | This is my Pandhari.
Says Tuka:
That is how it goes
When maya traps you in her throes.

SG

'Daughter-in-law, pay heed to what I say:
Go easy on the milk, don't use too much dahi.'
Did you think Mother-in-law was off to Pandharpur?
Oh no, she turned back at the border of the village.

'Listen well, my dear,' she said before going.
'That basin may be cracked but look after it.
My stack of cow pats? Leave it alone.
That pot of vermicelli? Hands off.
It's for making kheer.
I worry about my things, you know.
If a sadhu comes to the door,
Say, 'She's gone on a pilgrimage."
Eat in moderation. Not too much rich food.'

Daughter-in-law replies: 'Everything you say is right.
Now go on your pilgrimage with an easy mind.
Don't think of what you've left behind.'

But these very words sow seeds of doubt.
'Waiting for me to go, is she?
Why should I go on a pilgrimage?

What will I see there?
This is where my home is.
This is where my children are.
This is my Pandharpur.'

Tuka says: Thus the jaws snap
Of maya's trap.

JP

Mau mennaahuni aamhi Vishnudaasa

Mau mennaahuni aamhi Vishnudaasa | Kathhinna vajraasa bhedu aeese 1.
Mele jita aso nijoniyaa jaage | Jo jo je je maage te te deu 2.
Bhale tari deu gaandichi langoti | Naathhaallaache kaathhi deu maathaa 3.
Maayabaapaahuni bahu maayaavanta | Karu ghaatapaata shatruhuni 4.
Amruta te kaaya goda aamhaapudhe | Visha te baapude kadu kiti 5.
Tukaa mhanne aamhi avaghechi goda | Jyaache pure koda tyaache pari 6

We servants of Vishnu are soft as wax
Yet hard. We could split a thunderbolt.
Once dead, now alive. Asleep, now awake.
What people ask for, people will get.
For the good, we strip our backsides bare
The wicked get a stout stick on the head.
In love we outdo what your parents give
In rage we are worse than your enemy.
If nectar is sweet, we are sweeter still
Bitter poison is nothing to our ill-will.
Says Tuka:
We are sweet through and through
We will pamper you if that's your due.

SG

Vishnu's disciples are beeswax-soft.
We are rock that sunders Indra's bolt.

We were dead: we are alive.
We were asleep: we are revived.

For the good, even the langoti from our bums
For those who are bad, a stick to the head.

Our love is the love of your Mum and Dad.
Don't try us as enemies. We're surpassing bad.

Nectar has nothing on how sweet we are
Poison has no bitterness to compare.

Tuka says: We are sweet, all the way through.
But we also give each one their due.

JP

Bare jaale devaa nighaale divaalle

Bare jaale devaa nighaale divaalle | Bari yaa dushkaalle peedaa keli 1.
Anutaape tujhe raahile chintana | Jaalaa haa vamana sanvasaara 2.
Bare jaale devaa baaeela karkashaa | Bari hee durdashaa janaamadhye 3.
Bare jaale jagi paavalo apamaana | Bare gele dhana dhore gure 4.
Bare jaale naahi dharili lokalaaja | Baraa aalo sharanna tuja devaa 5.
Bare jaale tujhe kele devaaeela | Lekare baaeela upekshili 6.
Tukaa mhanne bare vrata ekaadashi | Kele upavaasi jaagaranna 7.

Good thing I am bankrupt, down and out.
Good thing this famine has struck me down.
Hardship has made me turn to you.
This world and its life I've vomited out.
Good thing my wife is a terrible scold.
Good thing I am thoroughly shamed in the world.
Good thing I'm tortured by people with taunts.
Good thing I feel no shame at all.
Good thing I'm left without cattle or wealth.
Good thing I'm at your feet all day.
Good thing I rebuilt your shrine.
Good thing I neglected children and wife.
Says Tuka:
Good I observed Ekadashi right,
Fasted and kept awake all night.

SG

I am bankrupt.
          Thank you for that.
This famine torments me.
          Thank you for that.
The world sickens me.
          Thank you for that.
My wife is a shrew
          Thank you for her.
I am a laughing stock.
          Thank you for that.
Money gone, and livestock too.
          Thank you for that.
I have no shame left.
          I'm glad of it.
          I am at your feet.
I neglected my family to restore your temple.
          I'm glad I did.
Tuka says: I celebrated Ekadashi just right.
                    I fasted and spent a wakeful night.

JP

Part Three

TUKARAM AND VITTHALA

Sundara te dhyaana ubhe vitevari

Sundara te dhyaana ubhe vitevari | Kara kataavari thhevuniyaa 1.
Tullasihaara gallaa kaase pitaambara | Aavade nirantara hechi dhyaana 2.
Makarakundale tallapati shravani | Kanthhi kaustubhamanni viraajita 3.
Tukaa mhanne maajhe hechi sarva sukha | Paahina shrimukha aavadine 4.

Oh this beauteous image!
Standing erect on a brick,
Elbows out, hands on hips,
Tulsi beads around the neck,
Waist girded in yellow silk.
Earlobes aglitter with rings
Forged in crocodile shape.
A kaustubh pendant winks
And sparkles on the chest.
This image I will adore
Now and forever more.
Says Tuka:
Here is my happiness
To gaze with love on this face.

SG

How beautiful you are, arms akimbo,
Standing on that brick,
Tulsi beads around your neck.
Your loins are girded in gold silk.

This is the form I shall ever adore.
Your earrings, crocodile-shaped, are radiant.
A kaustubh gleams at your throat.
Tuka says: Here is all my joy.
Your face, Your face.

JP

Hoya hoya vaarakari

Hoya hoya vaarakari | Paahe paahe re Pandhari 1.
Kaaya karaavi saadhane | Phalla avaghechi yenne 2.
Abhimaana nure | Koda avaghechi pure 3.
Tukaa mhanne dollaa | Vithho baeesalaa saavallaa 4.

Go on. Become a Warkari.
Go gaze on Pandhari.
No need to do anything more
You have what you are looking for.
Your pride is gone
You live to adore.
Says Tuka:
Dark Vitthal
Fills your eyes now.

SG

Be, be a Warkari.
Set out, set out for Pandhari.

What more do you need?
There you'll find all you seek.

Stripped of pride
All you'll want is to praise Him.

Tuka says: May Vitthal, the dark one,
Be in your eyes.

JP

Tujhyaa naamaachi aavadi

Tujhyaa naamaachi aavadi | Aamhi Vithho tujhi vedi 1.
Aataa na vajo annikaa thhayaa | Gaau geeta laago paayaa 2.
Kaaya Vaikunthha baapude | Tujhyaa premasukhaa pudhe 3.
Santa samaagama mellaa | Premasukhaachaa sukaalla 4.
Tukaa mhanne tujhyaa payee | Janmamarannaa thhaava naahi 5.

We are mad about you, we adore your name
All we want Vitho is to sing your praise.
Poor Vaikuntha pales before your presence.
Here we have bliss, in this gathering of saints.
Says Tuka:
At your feet,
Neither life nor death exist.

SG

Your name, Vittho.
Mad about it.

I need nothing else.
Just song. And your feet.

What could Heaven offer
More than your love?

This meeting of saints—
Bliss enough.

Tuka says: At your feet,
What's life, what's death?

JP

Chintile te maniche jaanne

Chintile te maniche jaanne | Puravi khunne antarichi 1.
Raatri na kalle divasa na kalle | Angi khelle daivata he 2.
Navasiyaache puravi navasa | Bhogi tyaasa bhinna naahi 3.
Tukaa mhanne samachi denne | Samacharani ubhaa ase 4.

He knows my thought, even as I think
He grants my wants, even as I wish.
I've lost all sense of night and day
God is in my body, we are at play.
Ask for boons, he responds
He becomes us in our pain.
Says Tuka:
Feet together on his brick
He gives to all, equally.

SG

He knows what I am thinking, all the time.
He gives me what I want, always.
In my body, when He's at play,
I lose all sense of night and day.
Ask for boons and you'll get them.
He's at one with the suffering.
Tuka says: His giving is even-handed.
Even his stance is balanced.

JP

Jethe jaato tethe tu maajhaa saangaati

Jethe jaato tethe tu maajhaa saangaati | Chaalavisi haati dharuṇiyaa 1.
Chaalo vaate aamhi tujhaachi aadhaara | Chaalavisi bhaara save maajhaa 2.
Bolo jaataa baralla karisi te neeta | Nele laaja dheeta kele devaa 3.
Avaghe jana maja jaale lokapaalla | Soeere sakalla praannasakhe 4.
Tukaa mhanne aataa khellato kautuke | Jaale tujhe sukha antarbaahi 5.

You are my companion wherever I go,
My hand in yours, you help me along.
I have your support at every step
I lean on you. You bear my weight.
When I blabber, you make it sense.
I was uncertain. You've made me brave.
The world has turned protector to me.
People are my beloved kin.
Says Tuka:
Full with the joy of you
My only delight is praising you.

SG

Wherever I go you are with me.
You lead me on. I lean on you.
We walk together. You bear my burden.
When I babble, you correct me gently.

Where I was diffident, you make me brave.
All the world's my friend.
Tuka says: Praising you is my play;
You suffuse me with joy.

JP

Bhetilaagi jeevaa laagalise aasa

Bhetilaagi jeevaa laagalise aasa | Paahi raatrandivasa vaata tujhi 1.
Poornimechaa chandramaa chakoraa jeevana | Taeese maajhe mana vaata paahe 2.
Divaallichyaa mullaa leki aasaavali | Paahaatase vaatuli Pandharichi 3.
Bhukeliyaa baalla ati shoka kari | Vaata paahe pari maaulichi 4.
Tukaa mhanne maja laagalise bhooka | Dhaavuni shrimukha daavi devaa 5.

My heart thirsts for a sight of you
All night, all day, I wait for you.
I am the chakor whose very life
Depends on seeing the full moon rise.
I'm the bride, longing for Diwali
And mother's home—her Pandhari.
The infant howls impatiently
Where is mother? He is hungry.
Says Tuka:
I too am famished. Cannot wait.
Rush to me Lord. Show me your face.

SG

All night long and the livelong day,
I long for you.
I long for you with the longing
Of the chakor for the Moon:
The longing for life itself.

I yearn for you
As a married girl yearns for Diwali
When she may go home again.
I yearn. I am a hungry child.
You, my mother.

Tuka says: I hunger. Come, come soon.
I need to see your face.

JP

Navhataa bheti tochi bare

Navhataa bheti tochi bare | Hotaa chore naadiyale 1.
Avaghiyaanchaa kelaa jhaadaa | Rita vaadaa khokara 2.
Chintanaache moolla chitta | Nele vitta haruni 3.
Tukaa mhanne mullaa aale | Hote kele taeesechi 4.

Life was good until we met.
The minute we did,
He stripped me clean.
Swept away all I had
Leaving me an empty shell.
The very seat of thought, the mind
Even that he took away
Says Tuka:
I'm back where I was
All my work till now erased.

SG

I had it good until I met Him.
He's a thief. He robbed me blind.
He ransacked my mansion
And took my prized possession.
He stole my mind.
Tuka says: I've been cut back to my roots.
He made me what I was.

JP

To maajhi maauli tu maajhi saauli

To maajhi maauli tu maajhi saauli | Paahato vaatuli Pandurange 1.
Tu maja ekalaa vadeel dhaakulaa | Tu maja aapulaa soyaraa jeeva 2.
Tukaa mhanne jeeva tujapaashi ase | Tujhiyaane osa sarva dishaa 3.

You are my mother, you my shelter
Pandurang, I wait in longing for you.
Brother of mine, older and younger
You are the beloved kin of my soul.
Says Tuka:
My life is with you alone
Beside you all else is barren.

SG

You are my mother and her breast.
You are the shade in which I rest.
You are the one I wait for
You, Pandurang, friend,

Revered elder, younger brother,
You're family.

Tuka says: My life is with you.
The rest means nothing.

JP

Gaato naachato aanande

Gaato naachato aanande | Taalla ghaagariyaachyaa chhande 1.
Tujhi tujapudhe devaa | Nenno bhaava kaeesi sevaa 2.
Nenno taala ghaata maata | Bhalate savaa paaya haata 3.
Laaja naahi shankaa | Preme ghaalo Tukaa mhanne Tukaa 4

I sing and dance with joy | To cymbals and ankle bells
Do I serve you God? | Don't know. I cannot tell.
I know nothing of beat | Or the sin of missing it
Without shame or doubt | I fling my limbs about
Says Tuka:
What's to be done?
Tuka is filled with your love.

SG

Clash of cymbals, clangor of ankle bells,
Tuka dances, he dances for you.
Is that what you want?
Is this service to you?
Can Tuka dance?
Fat chance!
No knowledge of rhythm, no feel for beat
Disaster awaits those two left feet.
Tuka's hands and feet thrash about.
He feels no shame, he feels no doubt.
Tuka says: Of this I am sure.
Whatever I do, you will love me still.

JP

Ekaa haati taalla ekaa haati chipalliyaa

Ekaa haati taalla ekaa haati chipalliyaa |
    Ghaaliti humbari eka vaataahaati taalliyaa 1.
Maatale Vaishnnava natati naanaa chhande |
    Naahi mokshapadi chaad bhajani aavadi 2.
Haakaa aarolliyaa geeta vaadya sukhasohalle |
    Jaaya te na kale kevhaa rajani divas 3.
Tithi naahi chaada na lage jaave vanaantaraa |
    Tukaa mhanne Hariharaatmakachi pruthivi 4.

Cymbals in one hand, castanets in the other,
The Vaishnavas are lost in their village games.
They clap, they call. They've gone quite mad.
They think up new tricks, new ways to play.
Ultimate salvation is no part of their aim.
No pilgrimage for them. No forest retreat.
All they want is to dance, sing and shout.
Day turns to night. They are beyond all that.
Says Tuka:
The earth is all Hari.
Hari to the brim.

SG

Cymbals clang, castanets click.
The devotees clap their hands.
Drunk on devotion, how they dance!
They sing out their praise.

They pour out their love.
This is here. This is now.
Mukti will take care of itself.
They shout. They rejoice.
Night falls and no one cares.
Day breaks and no one sees.
No need for forest retreats.
No pilgrimages or other feats.
Tuka says: It's all Hari.
               All of it: Hari.

JP

Aanandaache dohi aanand taranga

Aanandaache dohi aanand taranga | Aanandachi anga aanandaache 1.
Kaaya saango jhaale kaahichiyaabaaee | Pudhe chaali naahi aavadine 2.
Garbhaache aavadi maatechaa dohallaa | Tethichaa jivhaallaa tethe bimbe 3.
Tukaa mhanne taeesaa otalaase thhasaa | Anubhava sarisaa mukhaa aalaa 4.

The pool of bliss is rippled with bliss.
I don't want to move. I rejoice in this.
Indescribable, what's happened to me.
The pregnant mother craves the foetus' wants
An instant reflection of their bond
Says Tuka:
So it is with us
You are in me. My words, your reflection.

SG

Bliss is the pool
And the ripple, bliss.
How do I even describe this?
It defeats the imagination.
Whatever it is, I am transfixed.
The pregnant woman craves
What her baby needs.
Love binds them both.
Tuka says: You poured yourself into me.
These, your words, now break free.

JP

Durballaache konna

Durballaache konna | Aeeke ghaaluniyaa mana
Raahile kaaranna | Tayaavaachuni kaaya te 1.
Kallo aale anubhave | Paandurangaa maajhyaa jeeve
Na saangataa thhaave | Pado charyaa dekhoni 2.
Kaama krodha maajhyaa dehi | Bhedaabheda gele naahi
Hote tethe kaahi | Tuja krupaa karitaa 3.
He to navhe uchita | Nupekshaave sharanaagata
Tukaa mhanne reeta | Tumachi aamhaa na kalle 4.

Who listens to the weak with careful ear?
Nothing is lost if they remain unheard.
I know this Pandurang, in my very heart
Experience and your face, have told me that.
My body is still home to desire and rage.
I discriminate still between men and men.
I could be more deserving with your grace.
It is not fair that you turn away your face
From those who surrender and supplicate.
Says Tuka:
We fail
To understand your ways

SG

Who here hears the poor?
Of no account, they do not count.

No one had to tell me this.
I learned it from experience.
I divined it in your face.

Yes, I have angers. And desires.
I make distinctions.
I deserve no mercy.

But should you neglect those
Who surrender to you?

Tuka says: I don't understand
These ways of yours.

JP

Maajhyaa indriyaansi laagale bhaandanna

Maajhyaa indriyaansi laagale bhaandanna | Mhannateela kaana rasanaa dhaali 1.
Kariti tallamalla hastapaada bhaalla | Netraansi dushkaalla padilaa thora 2.
Gunna gaaya mukha aaikati kaana | Aamche kaaranna taeese navhe 3.
Darushanne phite netraanchaa to paanga | Jethe jyaachaa bhaaga gheteela te 4.
Tukaa mhanne aeese kari Naaraayannaa | Maajhi hi vaasanaa aeesi aahe 5.

My senses are at war | The ears say to the tongue
You've no cause to crib. | Limbs and brow despair.
Eyes without your sight | Suffer a dreadful drought
Tongue, ears, sing and hear | Leave the others out.
Give the eyes a glimpse | They've yearned for it too long
Let the rest choose | Take whatever they want
Says Tuka:
Do it Narayana
That's my wish. Just that.

SG

My senses make war on each other.
The ears complain: 'The tongue is happy.'
The tongue sings your praises. The ears listen.
The other organs fall to complaining.
The eye suffers under a drought.
My limbs and head are agitating.
The eye is easy to manage.

One glimpse of you will suffice.
But all the rest want to choose their part of you.

Tuka says: Do it for me, Narayana
That's the sum of my desires.

JP

Bare devaa Kunbi kelo

Bare devaa Kunbi kelo | Naahitari dambhe asato melo 1.
Bhale kele devaraayaa | Naache Tukaa laage paayaa 2.
Vidyaa asati kaahi | Tari padato apaayi 3.
Sevaa chukato santaanchi | Hechi naagavanna phukaachi 4.
Garva hotaa taathaa | Jaato Yamapanthe vaataa 5.
Tukaa mhanne thorapanne | Naraka hoti abhimaane 6.

Thank you, Lord | For my Kunbi birth.
High-caste cant | Would have been my death.
Tuka is saved. | He dances at your feet.
A bit of learning | Would have done me in
Stolen the solace | Of serving the saints.
What a great loss | That would have meant
Says Tuka:
The arrogance of proud men
Sends them down the path to hell.

SG

Thank you, God, for making me a Kunbi.
Born high caste, I might have died of hypocrisy.

You did well by me.
I dance and fall at your feet.

A little education might have spelt ruin.
I might not have served the saints for it.

This nakedness, this stripping?
It might have meant nothing.

Pride might have brought arrogance.
Arrogance, death.

Tuka says: Pride is the road
Big people take to Hell.

JP

Bhakti to kathhin shullavarila polli

Bhakti to kathhin shullavarila polli | Nivade to balli virallaa shoora 1.
Jethe paahe tethe dekhichaa parvata | Paayaavinna bhinta taatadichi 2.
Kaamaavale tari paakaa oja ghade | Ruchi aanni jode shlaadhyataa he 3.
Tukaa mhanne manaa paahije ankusha | Nittya navaa disa jaagrutichaa 4.

Devotion is baking bread on a stake.
The rarest warrior will submit to its call.
Wherever you look, false mountains soar,
And hasty walls without a base.
A dish is tasty, earns you praise
If you have slaved. Else it fails.
Says Tuka:
The mind needs a goad
To pierce it awake every day.

SG

To try bhakti
Is to roll rotis on the tip of a stake.
Bhakti is for the heart that is brave.

To try bhakti
Half-heartedly is to build illusions, walls
With no foundations, like far-off mountains.

To try bhakti
You must work on the dish and its savour.
Those who eat it will praise its flavour.

To try bhakti
Tuka says, is to pierce the mind with a goad.
And to do it again, again, every single day.

JP

Jivhaa jaanne phike madhura ki kshaara

Jivhaa jaanne phike madhura ki kshaara | Yera maasa para haataasa na valle 1.
Dekhaave netri bolaave mukhe | Chittaa sukhadukhe kallo yeti 2.
Parimallaasi ghraanna aeekati shravanna | Ekaache kaaranna ekaa navhe 3.
Eke dehi bhinna theviyelyaa kallaa | Naachavi putallaa sutradhaari 4.
Tukaa mhanne aeesi jayaachi sattaa | Kaa tayaa anantaa visaraleti 5.

The tongue knows insipid, sweet or tart.
The hand, though flesh, can't tell them apart.
The eyes have sight, the mouth has words
The heart knows the joys and griefs of the world.
The nose can smell, the ears can hear
Each sense unique, unlike all others.
Yet housed together in a single body,
They dance like puppets on His strings.
Says Tuka:
Infinite, omnipotent
How could You be so forgotten?

SG

Only the tongue is made to tell
What tastes salty, what tastes well.
Fashioned from the self-same stuff,
The hand would find tasting tough.
The eyes can see, the mouth can speak.
The heart knows joy, the heart knows pique.

You have ears to hear, a nose to smell.
Each organ does its own job well.
All this housed in a human frame
With a master puppeteer in charge of the game.
Says Tuka: With such power as His, I find it odd
How anyone could forget about God.

JP

Mana maajhe chapalla na raahe nishchalla

Mana maajhe chapalla na raahe nishchalla | Ghadi eki palla sthira naahi 1.
Aataa tu udaasa navhe Naaraayannaa | Dhaave maja deenaa gaanjiyele 2.
Dhaava ghaali pudhe indriyaache odhi | Kele tadaatodi chitta maajhe 3.
Tukaa mhanne maajhaa nachale saayaasa | Raahilo he aasa dharuni tujhi 4.

My mind runs amok. | Not for a second still.
Don't be aloof Narayana. | I am in torment. Run.
My senses ruin my peace | They force me to their will.
Says Tuka:
I have no recourse
But you. I cry for your succour.

SG

It won't stop, my mind, it won't stop.
But what do you care, Narayana?
Come a-running, save me.
My senses are killing my mind.
Tuka says: I can't do this alone.
My only hope is You.

JP

Karisi ki na karisi maajhaa angikaara

Karisi ki na karisi maajhaa angikaara | Haa maja vichaara padilaa devaa 1.
Desi ki na desi payaanche darshana | Mhannauni mana sthira naahi 2.
Bolasi ki na bolasi majasave devaa | Mhannoniyaa jeevaa bhaya vaate 3.
Hoeela ki na hoya tuja maajhaa aathava | Padilaa sandeha haachi maja 4.
Tukaa mhanne mi to kamaaeechaa heenna | Mhannauni seenna kari devaa 5.

Will you, won't you accept me? | I wonder and I worry.
Will you let me glimpse your feet? | The question unsettles me.
Will you, won't you talk to me? | Fear grips my heart.
Will you even remember me? | The thought tears me apart.
Says Tuka:
I've done so little, my Lord
That's the root of my fear.

SG

Will he accept me? Will he not?
I keep asking myself.
The reason my mind finds no rest:
Will he give me darshan of his feet?
The fear that haunts me:
Will you talk to me or not?
The doubt that plagues my soul:
Will you remember me or not?
Tuka says: I worry so much
For I have not done much.

JP

Vrukshavalli aamhaa soyare vanachare

Vrukshavalli aamhaa soyare vanachare | Pakshihi susvare aallaviti 1.
Yenne sukhe ruche ekaantaachaa vaasa | Naahi gunnadosha angaa yeta 2.
Aakaasha mandapa pruthivi aasana | Rame tethe mana kreeda karu 3.
Kanthaa kamandalu deha upachaaraa | Jaannavito vaaraa avasaru 4.
Hari kathaa bhojana paravadi vistaara | Karoni prakaara sevo ruchi 5.
Tukaa mhanne hoya manaasi samvaad | Aapulaachi vaada aapannaasi 6.

Creepers and trees are my kith and kin.
Birds too, warbling sweet melodies.
I'm happy. I like this solitude.
No one flings my flaws at me.
Sky is shelter. Earth is seat.
I'm free to play where I please.
A quilt, a waterpot, the body is served.
The wind tells me what hour it is.
Stories of Hari make a grand feast
To choose from, taste and relish.
Says Tuka:
My dialogue is with myself
All debates between me and me.

SG

These vines, these forest creatures are my family.
Those birds are my kin.
I can live among them:

No fault-finding here.
The sky my roof,
The earth my seat,
Here my mind is free to play.
A quilt, a water pot,
That's all I need.
The wind's way
Tells the time of day.
I eat stories about Hari
Savouring each mouthful.
Tuka says: Here I can talk with myself,
With time even for a quarrel or two.

JP

Tujhyaa rupe maajhi kaayaa

Tujhyaa rupe maajhi kaayaa | Bharo dyaavi Pandhariraayaa
Darpannichi chhaayaa | Ek rupe bhinnatve 1.
Sukha padile saathhavane | Sattaa veche shane shane
Adachanniche kona | Chaari maarga ugavale 2.
Vaso dollyaanchi baahuli | Kavalle bhinna chhaayaa aali
Krushnnaanjana chaali | Navhe parati maaghaari 3.
Jeeva thhasaavalaa shive | Manaa aale yethe jaave
Phaataa pahilaa naave | Tukaa mhanne khandale 4.

Lord of Pandhari, fill me with you
The mirror is false. It splits one in two.
With your joy in me, I've gathered strength,
Cleared every nook, all four paths freed.
My mirror once held a sickly face.
Since your blackness lined my eyes,
I have not seen that face again.
The eternal soul rules my body,
I'm free to wander where I please
Says Tuka:
We are one.
The breach that was, is bridged.

SG

Fill me up, Lord.
Fill my skin.

A mirror makes two
Where there was one.

I gather happiness
Bit by bit.

I rid myself of clutter,
Clearing every corner.

I looked in the mirror.
A wasted man looked back.

Now with Krishna for kohl,
That image vanishes, never to return.

Let the soul rule
And you're free to roam.

Tuka says: Yes, soul and body
Can be one.

JP

Lahaanapanna degaa devaa

Lahaanapanna degaa devaa | Mungi saakharechaa ravaa 1.
Aeeraavata ratna thora | Tyaasi ankushaachaa maara 2.
Jyaache angi mothhepanna | Tayaa yaatanaa kathhin 3.
Tukaa mhanne jaanna | Vhaave lahaanaahuni lahaana 4.

Neechapanna barave devaa | Na chale konnaachaahi daavaa 1.
Mahaapure jhaade jaati | Tethe lavhaalle raahati 2.
Yetaa sindhuchyaa lahari | Namra hotaa jaati vari 3.
Tukaa mhanne kalla | Paaya dharilyaa na chale balla 4.

God, grant me smallness | A sugar grain's enough for an ant
Gem of the ocean, Airawat, | Lord Indra's mighty elephant
Must still suffer agony | When the goad pierces his flank
The higher the man | The lower his fall
Says Tuka:
Understand
It's best to be smaller than small.

Humility is good my Lord | You make no enemies
A deluge uproots trees | But spares the lowly reed
Breakers come | The bullrush bends.
The breakers pass overhead.
Says Tuka:
At your feet
Might loses power. Suffers defeat.

SG

Give me smallness, my Lord
A grain of sugar to an ant.
Even Airawat the mighty,
Jewel of the ocean, Mount of Vishnu,
Must bear the goad.
Big is overrated.
Tuka says: Get this straight.
Small is good.

To be low is good, my Lord.
You make no enemies.
Trees fall in a flood, reeds survive.
When waves break, they pass
Over the back that is bowed.
Tuka says: What does your might count
At God's feet?

JP

Kaasayaa gunnadosha paaho annikaanche

Kaasayaa gunnadosha paaho annikaanche | Maja kaaya tyaanche unne ase 1.
Kaaya paapapunnya paaho annikaanche | Maja kaaya tyaanche unne ase 2.
Nashtadushtapanna kavannaanche vaanna | Tayaahuna annu adhika maajhe 3.
Kuchara khotaa maja konna ase aagallaa | To mi paaho dollaa aapuliye 4.
Tukaa mhanne mi yaa bhaandwala purataa | Tujasi Pandharinaathaa laaviyele 5.

Why point to another's flaws—
Are mine any the less?
Why count another's sins?
I have enough myself.
Why reproach evil in others?
None can match me there.
I know I am false and lazy.
Why scorn others like me?
Says Tuka:
My failings—my capital
I invest in you, Lord Pandhari.

SG

Why count the flaws in others?
I have a host.
Why point out the evils of others?
I have the most.
None so sinful as I

Whence deploy a suspicious eye?
Tuka says,
All the capital of my faults
I have invested in you, Pandurang.

JP

Laaja vaate maja maaniti he loka

Laaja vaate maja maaniti he loka | He to naahi eka maajhe angi 1.
Mojuni jhijalo maapaachiyaa pari | Jaallaavi he thori laabhaavinna 2.
Komalla kantaka teekshanna agari | Pochata te vari angakaanti 3.
Chitriche te lepa shrungaarile nike | Jeevevinna phike rupa tyaache 4.
Tukaa mhanne dise vaayaa gelo devaa | Anubhava thhaavaa naahi tenne 5.

I am ashamed at the world's acclaim
I've done nothing worthy of praise
To blazes with such hollow fame.
I'm like the measure that deals out grain
It wears itself out. Nothing retains.
A tender thorn has a pointed end.
Touch the point and see it bend.
Vivid hues that adorn a picture
Fade away if the picture's dead.
Says Tuka:
My life's a total waste
God, I do not know you yet.

SG

When people praise me, I feel shame.
Which grain scoop deserves any fame?
It must wear itself out in use.
These honours feel like abuse.
A green thorn has a sharp point, yes.

But that's all it has; no substance yet.
The colours in a picture matter not
Unless they live, they're just a blot.
Tuka says: My life has been a waste.
Of You, Lord, not even a taste.

JP

Taruvara beejaapoti

Taruvara beejaapoti | Beeja taruvaraa shevati 1.
Taeese tumhaa aamhaa jaale | Eki eka saamaavale 2.
Udakaa varila taranga | Taranga udakaache anga 3.
Tukaa mhanne bimbachhaayaa | Thhaayi paavali vilayaa 4.

The tree is born of the seed
The seed of the tree.
So it is with You and me
Entwined inextricably.
Ripples ruffle the stream
Both are equally water.
Says Tuka:
The object and image
Appear and vanish together.

SG

In every seed, the tree entire
At the end of every tree: the seed.

Tree: You. Seed: Me.

Tree: Me. Seed: You

The ripples on the water?
Water.

Tuka says: Object and image, present together;
Object and image, vanish together.

JP

Raatri divasa aamhaa yudhaachaa prasanga

Raatri divasa aamhaa yudhaachaa prasanga | Antarabaahya jaga aanni mana 1.
Jeevaahi aagoja padati aaghaata | Yeuniyaa nittya nittya vaaru 2.
Tukaa mhanne tujhyaa naamaachiyaa balle | Avaghiyaanche kaalle kele tonda 3.

Day and night, we are forced into battle—
With the mind within, the world outside.
The battering is brutal, the blows never end
Again they come, again we defend
Says Tuka:
Only the power of your name
Gives us strength to vanquish them.

SG

Battle stations, 24/7.
Enemy: The world.
Enemy: The mind.
Status: Barrage, constant, heavy.
Action: Fight back, stay vigilant.
Tuka says: Only your name
Can deflect this attack.

JP

Yaajasaathhi kelaa hotaa attaahaasa

Yaajasaathhi kelaa hotaa attaahaasa | Shevatachaa disa goda vhaavaa 1.
Aataa nishchintine paavalo visaavaa | Khuntaliyaa dhaavaa trushnechiyaa 2.
Kavatuka vaate jaaliyaa vechaache | Naava mangallaache tenne gunne 3.
Tukaa mhanne mukti parinnili novari | Aata divasa chaari khellimelli 4.

This is why I strove so hard,
To make my last day sweet.
The thirsty race is done at last
I'm free to rest. At peace.
I look back amazed at my gains
I took your name. Sang your praise.
Says Tuka:
Wedded to Mukti
My days are playful, free.

SG

I worked hard and long I strove
To make my last days sweet.
Now my peace has been won,
My thirsty race has been run.
I look back in wonder at my days
Of taking your name, singing your praise.

Tuka says: I have taken renunciation to wife
Ease will mark the rest of my life.

JP

Meechi maja vyaalo

Meechi maja vyaalo | Pota aapulyaa aalo 1.
Aataa purale navasa | Nirasoni gelo aasa 2.
Jaalo baaraaballi | Gelo maroni te kaalli 3.
Dohikade paahe | Tukaa aahe taeesaa aahe 4.

I have birthed myself | I have begotten me.
All my wishes granted | No desire left.
I became strong | The day I died.
Look both ways | Tuka is what he was.

SG

I give birth to myself.
I emerge from my womb.

Boons? Granted.
Desires? Vanished.
Naming? Done.
Body? Dead.

Tuka is as
Tuka was.

JP

Aapule maranna paahile myaa dollaa

Aapule maranna paahile myaa dollaa | To jaalaa sohallaa anupamya 1.
Aanande daatali tinhi tribhuvane | Saravaatmakapanne bhoga jaalaa 2.
Ekadeshi hoto ahankaare aathilaa | Tyaachaa tyaaga jaalaa sukaalla haa 3.
Phitale sutaka janmamarannaache | Mee maajhyaa sankoche duri jaalo 4.
Naaraayanne dilaa vasateesa thhaava | Thhevuniyaa bhaava thheli paayi 5.
Tukaa mhanne dile umatoni jagi | Ghetale te angi laavuniyaa 6.

I've seen my death with my very own eyes
What a celebration it was.
All three worlds spilled over with bliss
And I? I filled the cosmos.
I broke out of my puny self,
My paltry ego. Oh the joy!
Narayana made a place for me
I laid my love down at His feet.
Says Tuka:
His impress on the world
I have now absorbed into myself.

SG

I saw my own death. With my own eyes.
It was a blast. All three worlds dripped with bliss.
In the past, I was locked into my ego cell.
I cast that off, for this wide-open expanse.

I have let go of the narrow.
No more mourning over life, over death.
I dump all emotions at Narayana's feet.
Tuka says: He is stamped all over creation
And I have absorbed all creation into me.

JP

Annurennuyaa thokadaa

Annurennuyaa thokadaa | Tukaa aakaashaa evadhaa 1.
Gilluni saandile kalevara | Bhavabhramaachaa aakaara 2.
Saandilee triputi | Deepa ujallalaa ghati 3.
Tukaa mhanne aataa | Uralo upakaaraa purataa 4.

Small as an atom, Tuka fills the sky.
He has swallowed his corpse. Spat it out.
Shed illusion—form, content, the lot.
Cast off the trinity. Bid goodbye
To knower-knowable-known.
His body is aglow
With the flame of knowing
Says Tuka:
I am here now,
Only to render help.

SG

I am atom.
I am sky.
I eat my corpse.
I vomit.
I spurn maya.
I am done with the material.

All this business of 'Who knows-
Who is known-What can be known'?
I have no use for it.
Tuka says: Knowledge is a lamp inside me.
I burn now to help others.

JP

ALSO IN SPEAKING TIGER

INVOCATIONS AND PRAYERS OF KHWAJA ABDULLAH ANSARI OF HERAT

Translations by Sardar Sir Jogendra Singh and A.J. Arberry
Introduction by Syeda Saiyidain Hameed

A timely collection of Sufi prayers and counsels—that has travelled more than a thousand years—for our troubled times from one of the world's great mystics

Khwaja Abdullah Ansari—Pir-i-Herat, or 'Sage of Herat'—who lived in the eleventh century, is revered as one of the world's great and earliest Sufis. He turned to tasawwuf (Islamic mysticism) at a very young age, and came to be regarded as an extraordinary teacher, mystic, and an authority on Islam. Thousands were drawn to him and became his followers, and to this day his poetry and prose—collected in Persian and Arabic texts that are widely regarded as masterpieces—inspire and instruct scholars, seekers and the pious faithful alike.

Abdullah Ansari's tomb in Herat, in modern-day Afghanistan—a country ravaged in recent decades by discord and violence—remains a place of pilgrimage and peace for millions. In that beautiful sanctuary and elsewhere—including Panipat in India, where his descendants settled in the thirteenth century—his legacy and teachings continue to give solace to humanity, guiding us towards humility and compassion.

This compilation of Abdullah Ansari's invocations, prayers and counsels, selected from translations by two celebrated scholars, is a book of wisdom for all times. It is of particular relevance today, over a millennium after these words were spoken and recorded. As Syeda Hameed writes in her introduction, 'for our highly troubled and deeply hurt world, this is the healing hand of a wise Sufi Pir'.

INVOCATIONS AND PRAYERS OF KHWAJA ABDULLAH ANSARI OF HERAT

Translated by [illegible] ... Introduction by [illegible]

A [illegible] collection of Sufi prayers and [illegible] that has travelled [illegible] than [illegible] years [illegible] one of the world's great [illegible]

Khwaja Abdullah Ansari [illegible] of Herat, or Sage of Herat — who lived in the eleventh century, is revered as one of the world's great and [illegible] Sufi. [illegible] to this day his poetry and prayers [illegible] that the [illegible] regarded as [illegible] all.

Abdullah Ansari's tomb in Herat [illegible] Punjab in India, where [illegible] his poetry and teachings continue to give [illegible] to humanity, [illegible]

This compilation of Abdullah Ansari's [illegible] selected and translated by [illegible] is a book of wisdom for all [illegible] in her introduction, [illegible] healing hand of a [illegible]

ALSO IN SPEAKING TIGER

THE ANT WHO SWALLOWED THE SUN

The Abhangs of the Marathi Women Saints

Translated by Neela Bhagwat and Jerry Pinto

> '[A] splendid achievement. Neela Bhagwat and Jerry Pinto have rendered the luminous poetry of the women saints of Maharashtra's Bhakti movement into a persuasively cadenced English, as supple and robust as the original Marathi.'
>
> —Ranjit Hoskote, author of *I, Lalla: The Poems of Lal Ded*

The Bhakti movement, which began around the 6th century, transformed Indian thought in fundamental ways. It took seed in Maharashtra in the early 13th century in the form of the Warkari movement. With unmatched passion and eloquence the Warkari saint-poets spread the message of universal humanism, combining it with a deep devotion towards Vitthal. *The Ant Who Swallowed the Sun* is a collection of translations of abhangs by ten Marathi women-saints belonging to this movement.

These women came from diverse backgrounds: Muktabai was Saint Dnyaneshwar's sister; Janabai was Saint Namdev's maid, Rajai his wife and Gonai his mother; Bahinabai was a brahmin trapped in a difficult marriage; Kanhopatra was a sex-worker; Soyarabai and Nirmala were from lower castes; and not much is known about Bhagu and Vatsara. At a time when women hardly had any autonomy, each claimed Vitthal as their own, addressing him variously as the divine, the lover or the friend. Their abhangs are not just expressions of devotion but offer a scathing criticism of patriarchy and caste hierarchies. With Neela Bhagwat and Jerry Pinto's pitch-perfect translations, *The Ant Who Swallowed the Sun* is an important addition to Bhakti literature, as well as a delight for poetry lovers.